WRITING IN SMALL GROUPS

The 4color Way

by
June Gillam, Ph. D.

June Gillam

Published by Gorilla Girl Ink, USA

ISBN-10:
0-9858838-7-1

ISBN-13:
978-0-9858838-7-4

Copyright © 2017
By June Gillam, Ph. D.
Gorilla Girl Ink
All rights reserved.

www.junegillam.com
https://junegillam.academia.edu

Writing in Small Groups the 4color Way

Who is this book for?

Readers who want to be writers
Writers yearning to become better
Readers & writers willing to work in small groups

How does it work?

The book maps out a journey to improve writing skills inside the action cycles of Cooperative Inquiry's multiple ways of learning:

Ideas & concepts
Felt experiences
Artistic patterns
Practical activities

Along with Cooperative Inquiry (CI), the book invites people into a "4 color" process to expand ways of knowing so as to embrace vision, strategy, operations and outcome. In addition, the book offers "recipes" on how to assemble nourishing "sandwich" critiques for other writers.

June Gillam

My experiences in many CI groups, both face-to-face and online, plus that of my friends and students using these methods over the years, form the basis of this way of building writing power. Student comments include:

One thing I did in the past was to write solo without much input. I realized from my CI project how being part of a larger whole can uplift not just myself but others. It helps me stay motivated because when I share my writing with others, I feel it has purpose.

I find that using the 4colors, I can gather my personal goals, keep organized, reflect on my journey as a writer and help me push myself forward.

Being able to express what goes on in my own writer's mind, I created stories based off the troubles I've endured.

I liked the action cycles with the groups and having your peers read and give feedback on your work. I got to see a lot of different writing styles and different genres.

Sandwich feedback helped me get ideas from my fellow writers on how to improve my story with suggestions as to what I should include or touch up on.

The 4color journal has shown me I am a good observer, looking deeper into the meaning of things, and as a writer I am taking another step forward, sure that through writing I will see differently.

Writing in Small Groups the 4color Way

Who am I?

After earning an M.A. in English, I completed a Ph. D. In Transformative Learning and Change in 2003, focused on writing in a small group, and a Stanford Online Novel Writing Certificate in 2016. I recently received a Jack London Award in recognition of service to the California Writers Club for helping form the San Joaquin Valley Writers branch of the statewide organization, started in 1909 by Jack London and following this Mission Statement:

The California Writers Club (CWC) shall foster professionalism in writing, promote networking of writers with the writing community, mentor new writers, and provide literary support for writers and the writing community as is appropriate through education and leadership.

The club supports all genres, writing styles and related professions such as editing, publishing, photographic journalism and agents.

The branches provide an environment where members can obtain critique of their efforts, attend workshops, and share experiences. Branches are encouraged to mentor writers of all ages by providing educational programs for adults and fostering youth programs.

I've studied and worked for years to become a better writer and better support person for other writers. My own writing "disorienting dilemma," aka shocking realization that I needed to continue improving my writing, was when I came face to face with the fact that I, a published poet and good academic writer who taught college composition, could not write stories! I began to see that my problem was due to being raised in a home where conflict was off limits, yet conflict is the heart and soul of stories. I had been raised "story deprived" and felt compelled to tackle this problem. Through many years' effort and dollars invested, plus being in some powerful writing support groups, I overcame this obstacle and now have published short stories and a series of suspense novels. See Appendix A for my story.

This book is my way to share with others who feel frustrated and unable to create the writing they yearn to do. Details of my doctoral writing research project are set out in CREATING JUICY TALES: Cooperative Inquiry into Writing Stories, available in some libraries and at amazon.com.

Writing in Small Groups the 4color Way

What kinds of writing does this book address?

Any projects where people can form a group of two or more who are interested in the same topic. It's best with a leader, but it can work for self-organized writers, as well. Examples of the kinds of writing:

Essays

Short stories

Novels

Memoir

Life stories

Spiritual autobiography

Poetry

Journals

Other projects of interest

June Gillam

What is Cooperative Inquiry?

Co-operative inquiry is a way of working with other people who have similar concerns and interests as yours, in order to understand your world, make sense of your life and develop new and creative ways of looking at things learn how to act to change things you may want to change and find out how to do things better.

How does CI work?

Originally conceived by John Heron, a pioneer in the field of participatory research, CI is a system for people interested in learning about a topic to get together and form a question about the topic. Then they come up with a practical plan for each participant to go out and "test" the question by their actions. After the individual actions are complete, the group gathers back together, and each person presents what s/he did and what s/he learned. Finally, the group makes meaning from their combined experiences. These meanings are used as a basis for planning another action and reflection cycle, continuing in this circular way for as long as the group chooses. The individual person is always in interaction between what is going on inside the self and what is going on outside the self.

Writing in Small Groups the 4color Way

CI action-reflection cycles may include various ways of knowing:

> **Felt bodily senses, emotion**
>
> **Images and patterns such as in art & stories**
>
> **Intuition and sixth sense perceptions**
>
> **Learning ABOUT a topic**
>
> **Learning HOW to improve practice in a topic**

In the project for my doctoral research at California Institute of Integral Studies, I invited six women interested in the broad topic of "Writing Stories Containing Conflict" to join me to learn together rather than as isolated individuals. Paradoxically, I wanted to engage with other writers to experience feeling connected while writing alone; I wanted their support in facing my personal writing challenge, that of creating stories with characters in conflict. I hoped by collaborating in an interpersonal community, I might build my own intrapersonal community so all of us would nourish each other, embolden each other, challenge each other in striving to support our growth as writers. I wanted a writer's support group that went beyond assisting each other in writing to supporting our transformation as writers and human beings in the process of learning in a new and deeper way.

The outcomes of our inquiry were both individual and shared. Our main individual outcomes were changes in our inner beings as writers and in our writing practices and resulting stories containing conflict. We each wrote new stories over the course of the inquiry. Our main shared outcome was creating a "super" writing support group, similar to one of the guilds John Heron mentions here:

> The domain of the practical has [two] poles: individual skill and a culture of competence. At the heart of the former is an indefinable knack, and the essence of the latter is a felt ethos, a collective knowing how to value a whole body of practice, which also transcends verbal description. This knowing how to value shared competence is not an autonomous, individual knowing how in the way that a knack is. It is intersubjective, communal, the consequence of participating in a shared culture of practical excellence. The guilds of medieval craftsmen were, I believe, a focus for the affirmation, celebration and strengthening of this conjoint practical ethos (1996, p. 112).

In a nutshell, we created a learning environment for ourselves by way of a unique kind of writers' group, a Cooperative Inquiry group. By going through CI cycles, we encountered our personal obstacles and learned from them and in some ways, paralleled the processes of a character in a story. We continued to meet, write, and learn about ourselves as writers for nearly five years beyond the end of our formal inquiry for my dissertation.

Another outcome I hoped for was to facilitate other people to improve their craft at writing narrative, especially students in my creative writing classes. I believe this hope has been realized to an extent because many of my students have found tools such as the Hot Spot Grid

Writing in Small Groups the 4color Way

and the 4color reflections very helpful for them as writers.

Finally, I hoped my work could serve as a touchstone for adult educators of people seeking to recover stories and write them out, especially those containing the drama of conflict. Clearly, the CI method can be effective for college composition and creative writing classes, in addition to being useful for informal writing groups in the general population.

June Gillam

What is the "4color" way?

In THE POWER OF BALANCE: Transforming Self, Society, and Scientific Inquiry, William R. Torbert, creator of award-winning education programs, presents his idea that people live in four territories of experience. One way to think of these four colors, aligned with the working world, is that red is the same as the vision statement for an organization, blue is the strategy or plans, purple is the operations—what happens, and green is the outcome. I find it easy to memorize the four territories with this list which can be easily "translated" for various purposes:

Vision

Strategy

Operations

Outcome

In this book, I use Torbert's 4 territories as 4 points of view—4 colored windows—4 ways of looking at what we're reading, writing, discussing, and thinking about, so everyone gets a chance to see things from multiple perspectives, some they may not have thought of before.

These 4 territories welcome you to shift your habitual way to focus on a subject and its relationship to you—then see how your overall understanding changes. Thanks to Pennsylvania educator, Dr. Carol Welsh, for color-coding Torbert's 4 Territories.

Writing in Small Groups the 4color Way

Torbert's FOUR TERRITORIES through Welsh's FOUR COLORS:

RED—feelings, intuition, passion, desire, spirit, consciousness, mission, vision—You might ask yourself: **"What are my feelings, hunches, or intuitions about this?"**

BLUE—reasoning, planning, thinking, questioning, proving, quoting, critical analysis, strategy--You might ask yourself: **"What ideas or opinions do I have on this? What can I quote from the reading to support my idea of the meaning here?**

PURPLE—action, personal story, embodiment, behavior, operations--You might ask yourself: **"What personal experience have I had that is similar to this?"** or **"...very unlike this?"**

GREEN—the outside world, social and environmental issues, effect, rewards, impact, outcome-- You might ask yourself: **"What wider family, community, state, national, or international issues do I see reflected in this? Why is this important to the world?"**

Your 4color work will be uniquely your own--there is no right or wrong way to do it. It is simply a way to explore your creative thinking, feeling and reflecting processes.

June Gillam

Each time you work with the 4color tool, try to INCLUDE a balance of your

Intuitive, feeling responses (RED)

Thoughtful, analytical responses (BLUE)

Personal actions/story on the topic (PURPLE)

Connections to the outside, nature (GREEN)

The key is BALANCE AND AWARENESS. Also, it can be useful to end by reflecting on your process of using the 4 colors and what you learned from going through them.

Feel free to START IN ANY TERRITORY THAT SEEMS MOST NATURAL FOR YOU AND GO TO THE OTHERS IN THE ORDER THAT FEELS RIGHT OR MAKES THE MOST SENSE TO YOU.

Some people don't like to write to the "colors," and it's fine to just write freely BUT then go back to your writings and note the places where you see you were coming from the various territories. In other words, add in (Red) (Purple) (Blue) (Green) where ever you see yourself coming from each territory.

Writing in Small Groups the 4color Way

Here are my own ideas about the four colors, from CREATING JUICY TALES.

RED is bolded black, for access emotionally to my darkest passions, the other side of myself, swamped by the blinding light of my mother's positive nature, by the unreality of negativity stamped into my soul by Mary Baker Eddy, whom I took all too literally and yet not seriously as a woman of feelings herself; red, the color of the heat of my fire burning to find all 1000 of my shades of gray, red—short, blunt, to the gut, connected with how I feel, what drives me in what direction, juicy red.

BLUE is my cool reasoning process, what used to be so strong in my teacher persona, simply deliver the facts and direct the students (including myself) and they will write what is asked for, never asking who is doing the asking but taking the authority of "them" as solid, as a resting place for my heart, as the shell to cover the darkness of my stories, as a lightness to shine unquestionably, leading the pack with clear reasoning, how things should be, how to get to the painless land, a square and sad word, settled, dark gray, neither hot nor cold.

GREEN (I feel the least secure about green, feels like the most dependent on reflections from others, the most inner and outer mirroring, I feel most skeptical about green, most wary that there is any "one" theme, essence, truth, etc. I think this is due to my overdose of green in my abstract, conceptual Christian Science upbringing.) Green is the palest shade of gray, "light gray" in Word for me: I notice that the shape and sound

June Gillam

of the word itself is "greedy" maybe greedy to grasp "the truth" to set me free?

    PURPLE is the empty set for me, because I yearn for stories and cannot fill in the shapes of the words of the stories yet, but am committed to the pathway of learning how to; purple is the longest word in the four colors, a long slanted pathway for me, like climbing the Himalayas; it looks like it has many twists and turns, like either a maze I've been lost in or a labyrinth I'm finding the way to my center in.

Writing in Small Groups the 4color Way

What is "sandwich" feedback?

This is a method of offering responses to the writing of others in your small group. Imagine a sandwich—the bottom and top are usually bread. Think of the bread here as "praise." Start your response with praise and end it with praise—there is always something to appreciate in any writing. The sandwich filling is where to ask questions about what did not make sense for you and/or to offer tactful suggestions for changes that could help YOU as a reader enjoy the piece of writing more.

June Gillam

Until they realize what a gift honest reader feedback is, some writers do not want to accept others suggestions for changes to their writing. Below is a humorous cartoon showing the process of creating a sandwich critique—and getting resistance from the writer you are critiquing.

Request for permission is in process.

Writing in Small Groups the 4color Way

On the other hand, it's important to not make your critique too simplistic as shown here:

Request for permission is in process.

Be tactful. Come from your own experience as a reader—not as if you are the judge or a harsh teacher.

Be useful for the other writer in considering what to change in revision drafts.

All writers can benefit from learning to be open to others ideas about their writing. When in a group discussion and your writing is the subject of discussion, try to just listen. Think about what you might want to do by way of making changes after you get both the bread and the filling (questions/suggestions) about your piece of writing.

June Gillam

WHAT IS A GOOD SIZE FOR A CI GROUP?

"Groups of up to twelve persons can work well. Below six [can work but] might be a little too small and lack variety of experience" (Reason and Heron, Short Guide to CI).

So, at least four or five seems useful although best sizes can be between six and twelve. In my CI project, there were seven of us.

WHAT KIND OF TIME WILL THIS CI TAKE?

If you are in a college writing class, it could take eight to ten hours a week for 15 weeks, the length of a college semester.

(Generally 3 hours a week for the class meetings and 6-9 hours a week for your individual "homework," going by the Carnegie college units system.)

If you are in a different kind of group, it will depend on that group.

What kind of time do you want to give to it? (That is a good question for the "blue/planning" part of your 4color writers description.)

Writing in Small Groups the 4color Way

Your Turn—jot your feelings & ideas, etc., your responses—drawings, scribbles and words are all useful to write down here:

June Gillam

Why learn in this way?

This small group cooperative inquiry way is a process to teach yourself, a way to take responsibility for learning what you most care to find out. And to not only learn about it, but learn how to do it. Your way—along with others.

TEN STEPS FOR WRITING IN A SMALL CI GROUP THE 4COLOR WAY

1. Join a group looking into a topic you care about, for example "Improving Writing Skills"
2. Reflect on your own desires and dilemmas through a 4color process
3. Listen to others desires and dilemmas as they share their reflections
4. Take a role: leader, recorder, timekeeper, cheerleader, evaluator, etc.
5. Consider aspects of this topic & agree on a narrower topic formed as a specific question
6. Form a practical action plan in response to this narrower topic question
7. Individually carry out this action in the time between meetings
8. Share your experience and learning with the group & listen and learn from each other
9. Based on the group's learning, form the next action plan
10. Build a learning environment and continue the above steps for as long as it's fruitful.

THE TEN STEPS IN DETAIL

STEP ONE

Join an inquiry group on this topic.

Register for a class—this may start out as a large group, to be sorted into smaller units, depending on interests.

Go to a meeting of a group forming near you—this may be the right size to begin with or need sorting.

Sign up for an online CI project—there, too, the group may be the right size or need some sorting.

YOUR WAY

June Gillam

STEP TWO

Reflect on your personal desires and dilemmas. Write a 4color description of yourself as a writer. Include your:

Desires (red)

Plans (blue)

Actions to date (purple)

Outcomes, both good and bad (green)

Write by dipping your "pen" into the "four colors," so to speak. Consider these questions in shaping your writing about yourself through the four colors:

What are my hopes and dreams, my vision for myself as a writer? What do I want from this group? (red—your mission)

Do I have plans for myself as a writer? If so, what are they? (blue—your strategy)

What actions have I and/or do I take to manifest myself as a writer? (purple—your operations)

What outcomes have I achieved so far? What successes? What dilemmas? (green—your outcome)

HERE IS AN EXAMPLE OF A STUDENT WRITER'S INITIAL 4COLOR REFLECTION ON HERSELF AS A WRITER, FROM SPRING 2017

My vision for myself as a writer would be to write horror and erotic romance books. I love both and feel that I would be better writing more about books I love to read myself. I also have a few that I wrote and my husband read and commended me on, which furthered my need to do more writing since he is the hardest critic I know.

As of yet I do not have any major plans for myself as a writer except to just write more and actually try and get one of my books published. I do have a book in motion that I feel could possibly be a starter for me but I need to actually see it through. I feel doing that would get me closer to actually fulfilling some of my writing goals.

Some of the actions that I have taken to manifest myself as a writer would be the first step which I feel is actually having ideas, writing those ideas down and creating a storyline. I feel that this was the hardest thing for me because having so many ideas it was hard for me to pinpoint exactly where I wanted to start.

As far as my outcomes I'm not really happy because I feel that I could be doing more as far as writing a little more everyday and putting my notes together to actually finish something. With that said what I would like to get out of this course would be ways to help improve my writing and help me understand the basic and more complex concepts of creative writing.

June Gillam

Here's my 4color reflection as of June 9, 2017, as an example.

I dream of getting more of my suspense novels finished and published. I hope to get the best parts of my past writings collected, edited, and published including poems, memoir, ideas/essays and fiction. I hope to rewrite and reform some of my past published writings into ebooks and indie published books plus get more produced as audiobooks.

My current plans include finishing my fourth novel, House of Hoops, and getting it published as soon as possible, hopefully before the State Fair in July of 2018, so I can be there again in the Authors Booth.

I plan to write a brief version of my dissertation book and indie publish it through my Gorilla Girl Ink business.

I also plan to keep participating in writer critique groups and going to workshops and conferences. Learning all the time is exciting and essential for me.

Most mornings, my actions include that I write soon after arising, meditating for ten minutes, and having coffee. I usually have at least one writing project going at a time. I have two places I write in: upstairs on my iMac desktop computer for my blogs or downstairs in the dining room on my MacBook Air.

Writing in Small Groups the 4color Way

Most evenings I read for about an hour, usually fiction but often non-fiction as well. Right now I'm reading THE GIRL ON THE TRAIN by Paula Hawkins, DEAD WEIGHT by T. R. Ragan, and OF WOMAN BORN by Adrienne Rich.

I have boxes and file drawers full of writing plus loads of computer files, too. I've been published in student newspapers and magazines, in online magazines, in small literary magazines, in an academic press, and via my own independent publishing company, Gorilla Girl Ink. I have joined and/or co-created writing support groups since the late 1970s, including The Sacramento Feminist Writers Guild. I have degrees earned by way of various kinds of writing. I am teaching writing keeping in mind and heart the philosophy I first heard back in the early 1990s from my colleague who taught Speech: we are all teaching what we most need to learn.

I am happy with some of my outcomes because they express my own truth in various ways. I am also not happy with them because they don't seem to have gathered many readers yet, so I want to learn more on book distribution and marketing.

BACK TO YOUR TURN

Continue writing, coming to focus on your own connection to the topic of "Improving Writing Skills" and share with the group. Describe your desires, plans, actions and outcomes. Include your problems, your disorienting dilemmas regarding writing.

Writing in Small Groups the 4color Way

STEP THREE

Listen to others desires and dilemmas; regroup together with people who have similar issues to form smaller units.

Pay attention to what you have in common with others in the group. Doodle or sketch images as you listen for rich awareness.

Optional: Add to a collaborative image by the group to tap into non-worded knowing/feelings; stand back and reflect on what you see in the images towards zeroing in on a narrower topic question.

STEP FOUR

Take a role: leader, recorder, timekeeper, cheerleader, evaluator, etc.
Notice what the various roles do for the group. Consider your experience and temperament and how you can best support your small group.

Leader—keeps the group focused on the steps of a CI, getting it done.

Recorder—takes notes on what happens in the group, how the plans form.

Timekeeper—helps the group stay focused on getting the job done in the time available.

Cheerleader—boosts everyone's spirits.

Evaluator—reports the ways the group got its action plan completed in each cycle.

STEP FIVE

Form a narrower topic based on specific questions. Consider questions on the writing element you most want to improve at this time. Some possibilities:

What are my strengths and weaknesses as a writer?

What most helps me and hurts me in writing?

How do writers I admire go about their writing?

How can I write in response my reading?

How can I write a compelling blog post?

How can I write good poetry?

How can I push past procrastination/writers block?

How can I write in a genre? (pick one)
- **Adventure**
- **Romantic Suspense**
- **Psychological Suspense**
- **Thrillers**
- **Horror**
- **Mysteries**
- **Science Fiction**
- **Fantasy**
- **Historical Fiction**

June Gillam

STEP SIX

Form a limited, practical action plan.

Think about the questions offered by the group, and narrow them down to one that best fits the sense of the whole group. It could be valuable to separate the group into smaller units at this time, depending on interests.

Then form a practical action plan for each individual to carry out when away from the group, which would respond to the narrower question members showed interest in. Make your plan the right "size" for the time between meetings. Give yourselves not too much nor too little to do. Include ideas on ways for you as individuals to keep track of what you do.

Example from CREATING JUICY TALES: Our first cooperatively formed action plan was to

(a) start and finish something or finish something already started

(b) keep track of, record, individual actions and process by way of journals, drumming, artwork, etc.

(c) be ready to present to the group on what we did, plus showing our recording method or simply telling about it.

Writing in Small Groups the 4color Way

STEP SEVEN

Individually do the action in the time between meetings.
Each group member independently carry out the action described in the plan and keep track of what they did.
An **example** of how I did one of the action plans in the Creating Juicy Tales project:

Our plan was to write a story by "springboarding" from "Seven Meaningful Concepts" about creating conflict we had generated from what we'd learned.

Soon after our meeting, I began gazing at the list of seven concepts and was initially drawn to the idea that it could be useful to search for what feels conflicted. I liked the idea of what felt juicy, what had an embodied aspect to it. I imagined a character who craves something, consciously or unconsciously, and feels a growing, energetic, and even dangerous external obstacle and a more subtle but growing inner obstacle to getting what she increasingly knows she must have. I envisioned someone who keeps struggling toward what she wants in the face and body of confronting obstacles, inner and outer, using her force that is growing in energy as she comes to feel up against the forces of the obstacles. I wrote lists of names of people I know, speculating on what they truly want, in order to practice this idea of focusing on what people deeply desire.

I felt connection with our concept that the many character aspects within ourselves are sources for story characters and also that we used both inner and outer conflict in the stories we had presented last meeting. I searched for inner character aspects within myself, looking for something with a lot of feeling from my life to use as a source. I found a memorable, emotional climactic "snapshot" from childhood which I "relocated" to an outdoor setting, to give myself a fresh perspective on it.

To keep focused on conflict, I tried to write a minimalist scene of 200 words or so that would be just the conflict, in present time so as to move the action quickly, getting to use the shortest form of the verbs, and striving for a rhythm of "right now and right now and right now." I wrote out the dialog and the actions, as sparse as I could get them. In order to stay with the feelings, I used the real childhood names. Because I only knew what the climactic ending was, I was creating from my imagination all the dialog and action leading up to the climax. As I was writing along, I noticed that as we had discussed in our meeting, writing conflict felt like making love, that the game is to prolong the sensation, to build the tension to the extreme, so when you get to the climax the release will be most fulfilling. This process resulted in a story I called "Monopoly," about two sisters playing that popular board game out in the blazing California Central Valley summer sun.

I kept expanding this story, reviewing our seven concepts from the previous meeting, and even the definitions of conflict we had created in an earlier meeting. I saw that "Monopoly" touches on the "power/victim" and the "shadow side/mask" polarities

Writing in Small Groups the 4color Way

of our first Cooperative Inquiry definitions we had created together as our first understanding of "Conflict Evolution." I saw too that the story "Monopoly" contains both inner and outer conflict—the outer conflict was over which sister would win the Monopoly game. The older sister's inner desire to be a mature good sport, "above" petty anger, constructs her character mask. On the other hand, her inner desire to win, to show she's the smartest, comes from her shadow side and is in inner conflict with her mask side. She is jealous of but powerless over her younger sister's quick wits; she is the victim of her younger sister's honest competitive desire, unconflicted by a mask of "goodness."

Again, near the end of this action cycle, I felt called to draw a 4-color reflection on my process and its meaning. First it came to me to draw three red hearts, representing my sister, myself, and a third sister who was not in the "Monopoly" story. Red is the feeling color, conveying both love and anger, anger in my family and among my two sister characters. Then I drew many small crosses in blue to represent the reasonable, nice girl, lady-like ways my sisters and I were taught to act, such as crossing our legs when seated, folding our hands in our laps; those are peaceful, "tucked up neatly," rational images. I think they looked like birds flying around in the air, yet not free, but rather burdened by being crossed.

After reflecting on this hearts and crosses drawing, I realized that what got left out were purple and green, which represent embodied action/personal story and outcome/outside world. These omissions were so

June Gillam

appropriate because that's how it is in our family, we're all lovey dovey hearts on the surface, and close emotionally, yet we don't have stories, no purple in our family, our family has no stories.

It hit home: I realized that in my life what I remember are the climaxes, those intense bursts of feeling, like snapshots. I noticed I had tended to put out of my mind, or was never aware of, all the small actions, the tensions and conflicts, that lead up to the climax. I had no moving pictures of the stories. The colorful drawing helped me to see the reality of having no stories, yet ironically this insight was in the midst of writing the "Monopoly" story itself.

See Appendix C for the short story "Monopoly" that was published in *Metal Scratches: A magazine of short stories*, Issue 5, 2005.

Writing in Small Groups the 4color Way

STEP EIGHT

Return to the group and share individual experience and learning with the group.

Examples from CREATING JUICY TALES: (I used pen names for privacy except for myself who is the "I" in this report.)

Kate showed how she'd kept track of her process in a literal "little journal," an artful and colorful creation made of green 3x5 index cards on which were glued cutouts from computer printouts describing what she did and where on each of the days between meetings. Each page had tiny stickers in the shape of hands to represent her actual work, her actions. She had thought of revising her short story "Pat Reilly" but chose instead to revise her autobiography, adding in material about her mother, which she then read to us.

Lilly presented a large collage, tied into a scroll with purple ribbon. She unrolled the collage and posted it to an easel, giving us some time to simply gaze and "make sense" of it for ourselves. She then told the story of her process, pointing to various images arranged in a symbolic "story" created from her computer scannings of real flowers. The materials on the board conveyed Lilly's story of the action she completed, in which there was a major and minor family conflict, with various characters in the story depicted by specific flowers juxtaposed both together and scattered. I noted that the path of the actions looked like a right brain artistic version of a common upward sloping path to illustrate the uphill path of a character experiencing conflict in plot.

    I went next and showed the way I had kept track of my action to create a plotline in the shape of an upward pointing and zigzaggy arrow for one of my short stories that lacked conflict. I kept track of the stages of my process by creating various rhythms on a drum, which I played for the group on the small drum I brought to the meeting. I showed my "arrow" and explained it and how it was similar to Lilly's "flower flow" story of her own dramatic narrative process.

    Bridget then showed how she kept track of her action, which was to renew her teaching credentials. In a small album, she'd glued a silhouette of a ringmaster holding a hoop with a dog jumping through it: the ringmaster was the State of California Credentialing Bureau and she was the "dog" jumping through bureaucratic hoops, with another dog nearby, representing her school principal, who supported her in finishing her action. Bridget showed a collage of photographs of her students she'd arranged against a blue sky with clouds and explained that her students were why she'd been willing to jump through bureaucratic hoops.

    Petunia stood up to pantomime thinking about her action and typing at an imaginary computer with a happy expression, her expression later giving way to frustration and then disgust. She mimed repeatedly wadding up paper and throwing it away, then began clutching her jaw and grimacing in pain, then taking pills and swallowing with water. Next, she pantomimed dialing and talking on the phone, while rubbing her jaw and her stomach with a pained look on her face. She then verbally explained she had begun to work on a video script of her life but had been dragged down by the pain of a bad tooth, and had to have surgery on her jaw.

Star represented her action with a series of melodies, sounds, and movement, sitting on one side of her chair then the other, depicting her interactions internally and with other persons. After she completed her series of sounds and movements over a few minutes, she verbally explained her intended action had been to apply to teach English at a private college in Stockton. Star told the story of her aggravations in completing a resume and making a series of phone calls, at first getting turned down then later being called in for an interview by a dean, culminating in being hired to teach Contemporary Literature starting in the fall.

Marcella told of her struggles to complete some crocheted handwork in time for a baby shower. Although she did complete the project, she was not able to bring it to our meeting because it had to go to the baby shower that morning. So that she would have something to present for us, Marcella had started and finished a stunningly realistic cream-colored silk rose complete with stem and leaves, that she made into a pen and presented to me.

STEP NINE

From the group's learning, form a new action plan. **Example** from CREATING JUICY TALES:

Over time, our action plans for writing stories became more specific, creating a richer and more fertile environment for research into transforming our writing abilities. Our key action plans were four story writing assignments we gave ourselves. We had first asked the broad question: "How do you write a story containing conflict?" For our first action we planned to "Write a story containing conflict and to keep track of our process."

After we presented the outcomes of our Labor Day meeting and reflected together on what we'd learned, seven meaningful concepts about writing stories with conflict emerged and we wrote them on easel paper. For the next round of stories, we planned to "choose one or more of the seven concepts to focus on and springboard from that to write a scene or story."

In that sort of way, each new plan was based on what we'd learned from our previous individual actions. See Appendix B for a table showing our action plans and story outcomes.

STEP TEN

Build a learning environment. Following are eight ideas with **examples** of ways to do this, from CREATING JUICY TALES:

1. DEVELOP WRITTEN GROUP NORMS to ensure a safe group space, include how to handle processing emotional distress. We agreed on six "Ground Rules For Safety In The Group" (See Appendix A), which included that ideas/opinions/writings can be criticized but not the person and that we all had the right to reveal only as much as we chose to, or simply to pass. Create a safe setting that lets us show our vulnerable selves in our writing processes and outcomes. Keep interpersonal conflict under control in group process in ways such as avoiding it, playing at it, and/or taking it up in a rational discussion way. Some areas in which we let conflict "out" into the group space were in our vocal conversations exploring our sensitivity to criticism, the thinness or thickness of our skins.

2. CREATE YOUR OWN "ASSIGNMENTS" by your action plans. In addition to building a safe setting that allowed us to grow in trusting each other with our author's vulnerability, our creation of assignments and our service as listeners/readers of each other's stories facilitated the continuing improvement of our writing abilities. A big impact on our individual writing processes was having created our unique series of action plans together, in line with the Cooperative Inquiry methodology. We gave ourselves what some of us called "assignments," which in many ways were both permission at the same time they were directions to write stories with conflict. Having this ongoing "outside" stimulus--which had not really come from outside ourselves but rather from inside the whole group--was a significant factor for all of us as we experienced the regular rhythms of writing alone and reflection together when we met.

3. GIVE USEFUL FEEDBACK

In our feedback, we were supportive of each other's work and truthful as well. Most often, we adopted a convention of addressing the stories as if they were fictional, but many times they were true life stories, so we kept a fuzzy line between reality and fiction.

At first, our learning in the group was more at the level of simple strategies picked up at our meetings: "The feedback you all gave me in terms of putting more in so the reader can really hear what the conflict is or where it's taking place and how come it's happening, what were the obstacles--I would not have thought of writing that way before," said Petunia.

Sometimes we realized what useful tips for our individual writing processes we were getting from each other in the round-robin flow of our conversation: "I like what you said about writing the story, maximizing the conflict making it even more than it was," Petunia told me.

"And I like your question," I said to Lilly, "What's the worst thing--how did you phrase that?"

"What's the worst thing that you could imagine happening to you," she replied. I noted I had modified that to what is the worst conflict you can imagine. "Right," said Lilly, "I was talking about this to a couple of friends and we were getting into it--just having the conversation started getting us all chilled out, because that's what a Stephen King imagination does."

We looked forward to hearing what "we" had done individually. Our writing processes were stimulated by the audience of our group awaiting our presentation of what we'd done and produced. As Petunia put it, "Having a group of people looking forward to what I was writing was a positive pressure to complete what I promised by a certain date--it was nice to know I had an audience!"

"I know honestly I wouldn't have written some of the stories I wrote if I didn't have an audience for it," said Marcella.

"It's just the action of having to actually produce something that motivates me to go for my edge," said Lilly, "'cause I don't want to let the group down or let myself down as part of the group."

At times our feedback sessions seemed to reveal some of our inner writing dynamics we hadn't seen before and give us permissions we may not have been aware we needed as keys to transforming our writing. "You took in everything everybody said from the last meeting about really bringing in the conflict and going beyond yourself," Petunia acknowledged Lilly.

In addition, we explored the qualitative range of our feedback to each other's stories, from politeness through harsh criticism. "I think in this group we're just being nice to each other," offered Star in a conversation early in our work together.

"I don't feel like I've been nice or not nice," Bridget said. "I don't feel like I've held back on any criticism of any stories, and so then I start thinking gosh maybe I don't know how to criticize very well, because I haven't had the desire to be not nice--"

"I don't think it's 'nice or not nice,'" Lilly interjected. "I think all of it is a way of giving positive critique, even including negative comments on the story."

"Well, I mean critique with some sensitivity that this is the person that's sitting here listening to you," said Bridget. "Back to the word 'nice.' I mean you can say it in a way that allows the person to have dignity."

"Right," Lilly agreed.

"I don't care if you tell me it stinks, if you tell me where and why, that's a gift," said Petunia. "I feel anything you tell me is a gift, even if you don't say it politely. I mean, it may hurt but I'll live, and maybe it couldn't be said any other way at that particular moment--it's a gift that somebody would share with me what they think."

"Well I'm an extremely sensitive person," said Bridget. "I guess I was wondering well what is conflict anyway, is it being harsh to each other? Is it being rude to each other? I don't think so, I mean I work in a classroom with disabled children who know how to be rude to each other but is there any real conflict there?" She started to explain her approach to polite critique that still makes a point.

"What's polite?" said Petunia.

"There's a good point," said Bridget. "What is polite?" she echoed Petunia's question.

"I just interrupted you, was that impolite?" Petunia inquired.

Here as elsewhere, some of us played with conflict as a way to approach it: "Oh, I'm going to go home and cry," Bridget said, laughing.

"Well, you may be polite but that doesn't mean the person you're talking to is going to think you're being polite," Star said to Bridget, "so it depends on that other person, also."

"That's true, too," agreed Bridget. "Politeness comes from--"

"Culture," Petunia contributed.

"Cultural things, family things," Bridget said. "I think in this group we can kind of--"

"I think we should take some risks," Lilly interrupted.

"I think you did take a risk, Petunia said to Lilly, "in your writing; I guess I'm in the mood to go in and do some critique or talk about the writing."

"I think we are ready," said Kate. Much of the inquiry into conflict in our study came through our attempts to both show it in our writing and give feedback on conflict's presence or absence in our stories, more so than in our group process dynamics, in my view.

4. NOTICE THE RELATIONSHIP OF WRITING TO VULNERABILITY

In the early phases, we had a pattern of stalling, of putting off presenting our stories because we did not yet trust each other with our vulnerable writer selves as much as we would near the end.

"And also whenever we talk about our own writing process and our own stories, we're making ourselves vulnerable," Marcella observed, and Petunia agreed. "And it's--" Marcella continued.

"Scary," Petunia finished the thought.

"That's right," Lilly agreed.

"That's what's hard about making ourselves get right to our stories," I added and Lilly agreed.

"Whenever you talk about how you write and about your own story," Marcella said, "you're making yourself vulnerable."

"Sure," Petunia said.

Marcella continued, "And it's a defense reaction to delay it as much as physically possible." There was general agreement in the group.

"I think there's a lot of truth there," I said.

"So let's not do that anymore," Star laughed.

"I think maybe we have unconsciously helped ourselves by putting ourselves into a compressed space time tonight, do you think?" I asked.

"Yeah," Star agreed, "I think it helps--"

"But even so, we spent the first hour talking," Marcella countered, "and then extended our time an hour until ten."

I answered, "Well maybe we need the postponing getting into our stories to reestablishing our feeling of comfort or something?" This felt right to many of us.

5. BE PATIENT—TRUST AND SKILLS TAKE TIME TO BUILD

Our ongoing cycles of meetings helped us build more trust in each other and the process, so we became more comfortable being vulnerable by way of exposing our writing processes and outcome to each other.

AND BE PATIENT WITH WHAT FEELS CHAOTIC

"The inquiry process is a bit like. . . . the self-organizing dynamic of a complex system that gets itself to the edge of chaos and then emerges at a higher level of complexity" (Heron, 1996, p. 148). Tolerating chaos as it evolves into new levels of order is considered valuable in a Cooperative Inquiry, so as to not close off emerging meaning before it has had time to rise and form into concepts; Heron says "this is not so much a procedure as a mental set which allows for the interdependence of chaos and order" (1996, p. 60).

We built up more assertive leadership skills in the service of the whole group as we went along. After the Labor Day agony in time lock, we became more outspoken at keeping ourselves to our agendas. For example, once when it came time for Star's story, I was showing how her Emailed printout version of it had looked. I said to a couple of women, "You can see how it prints out for me, so we can get a better sense of each others--"

Petunia, as timekeeper that evening, broke in to address me. "You are wasting somebody's time right now."

"Okay," I accepted her support to stay on time. Later, Kate asked if anyone wanted some "little chocolate candies" she had in the other room.

"Taking away from time for Star," Petunia warned.

We became bolder in taking up time when it mattered, rather than going along with the group just because it was easier or quicker. Once, when we were discussing our next action, the group seemed to be coalescing around the question Bridget had offered, "How do you acquire courage?" with the possible corresponding action being to "write a story where a character acquires some courage." Petunia tested our consensus: "Very good! all right? Everybody?"

"Actually I don't particularly like it but I'll go with it," Bridget stated.

"I cannot relate to that for five seconds," Kate said to loud laugher in the room.

"Neither could I," admitted Bridget, "but I'm just going with the flow."

"I don't want to be difficult but that question and plan give me nothing," Kate said. "What do they mean?"

"Well, maybe you will find a meaning," Petunia responded to Kate. "When I'm thinking about something, I like to not 'worry wart' it but to live in the question of it. The meaning doesn't always come when I expect it, it might come on the freeway, or I wake up with it," Petunia said, going on to advise the group to "struggle with it, have the courage to struggle" with the proposed question and action plan to write a story where a character acquires some courage.

"It could be any character--" I said.

"Who starts with no courage and gets it," Petunia interjected.

"Because built into that plan is some kind of scary thing they have to face, so that's their conflict, right?" I asked. I heard no agreement nor disagreement to my question, and I said directly to Bridget: "Well, don't just say 'Yes' you want to do it just to get it over with." A couple people nodded their agreement we should not be hurrying through the process.

"No, I didn't say that," Bridget replied.

"I thought I saw that in your eyes," I said to loud laughter and voices.

"You're not a mind reader," Petunia said.

"Well I know," I countered, "I'm just saying I thought I saw that--"

"You said you saw it in her eyes," Petunia interjected.

"I said I thought I saw it in her eyes," I said.

"I came up with that question just because of my linear thought patterns," Bridget said, "and I'm willing to go with it, but if somebody has a different idea I'm willing to go with that too."

"It is now ten o'clock," Petunia stated.

"Kate what were you going to say?" asked Lilly, opening us back up to Kate's earlier voiced concerns that she could not relate to Bridget's proposed question and action plan under discussion.

"I just I can find more meaning when we say conflict is fear," Kate said. "Really we are afraid of how our husband will act or how our brother or our neighbor will act, so that's conflict." There was general agreement on this point.

June Gillam

Because of our willingness to engage in mild, but authentic conflict in our conversation, we shifted our question and action plan for our next cycle from exploring acquiring courage to exploring how fear produces conflict and asking if it does. However, our diverse views were processed quite rationally with slight emotional charge. It was clear that much of the time, we let our stories and our feedback on stories do our emotional distress work rather than doing it in our group process.

We built and continued to thrive in our safe yet challenging transformative learning environment. Our willingness to play Devil's advocate for one another and our patience during periods of swirling chaos in the group reflection sessions contributed greatly to the effectiveness of our group process for us. Rather than confronting and processing emotions in our group, we seemed to shift that part of Cooperative Inquiry over to how emotions were manifested or suppressed inside the dynamics among the characters in our stories and inside ourselves during our individual writing processes, which seems very appropriate for the topic of this particular study.

6. BE WILLING TO ENGAGE IN TRANSFORMATIVE LEARNING

Transformative learning is not simply the learning of some new content or skill, although it may include that. Instead, it is learning about the self as a learner, seeing formerly hidden assumptions and beliefs that blocked understanding of one's process of learning. Of the various schools of thought on what constitutes transformative learning, three seem to be closely associated with the topic of this book.

BLUE: transformative learning by enlarged cognitive understanding through a person's rational ego, described by Jack Mezirow (1991, 2000) in his teaching and writing in the field of adult and continuing education.

RED: "transformative education" conceived by educators Robert Boyd and J. Gordon Myers (1988) in a Jungian approach to transformative learning, which includes focus on multiple aspects of a person, including the emotions.

PURPLE: ability to do an action, as distinct from a person's learning about a topic under study. John Heron (1996) writes that he gives primary importance to practical knowing over theoretical although he values both.

CONSIDER VARIOUS WAYS OF TRANSFORMING THE SELF AS A WRITER

As presented by educator and scholar Jack Mezirow (1991), transformative learning means an enlarged cognitive understanding, a rational reframing of a person's "meaning perspective." By this term, Mezirow (1991) means a person's worldview and cluster of meaning schemes, which he believes can operate as a filter below the level of awareness, keeping a person stuck in old habits which may no longer serve him or her. Mezirow has been criticized by others in the field as overly rational (Taylor, 2000), although Mezirow (2000) has lately woven in a bit more attention to emotional and spiritual aspects than he had earlier (1991).

In order to later compare and contrast what occurred in our study with Mezirow's (2000) approach, and including the caveat that Mezirow does not offer these stages as mandatory, mechanical, "lock-steps" in any way, I list here his ten "phases" of transformative learning:

1. A disorienting dilemma
2. Self-examination with feelings of fear, anger, guilt, or shame
3. A critical assessment of assumptions
4. Recognition that one's discontent and the process of transformation are shared
5. Exploration of options for new roles, relationships, and actions
6. Planning a course of action
7. Acquiring knowledge and skills for implementing one's plans
8. Provisional trying of new roles
9. Building competence and self-confidence in new roles and relationships
10. A reintegration into one's life on the basis of conditions dictated by one's new perspective (p. 22).

Writing in Small Groups the 4color Way

The emphasis in Mezirow's (2000) approach is transformative learning for the individual adult learner in a group setting. The role of the group in Mezirow's approach seems to be to provide an arena in which rational discourse can flourish, in which each person can learn by listening to others in a respectful and yet critically reflective way, working to come to conceptual truth for his or her autonomous self. "The ideal of a graduate seminar" is pointed to by educator Mezirow to "serve in some respects as a model of group discourse [having] no outside coercion. . . equal opportunity to contribute. . . norms of courtesy, active listening, studying issues in advance, and taking turns to talk" (p. 15).

In this approach, the group appears to be led by an adult educator. Regarding power issues in the group, Mezirow (2000) believes that adult educators should create safe "protected learning environments" to bring about "conditions of social democracy necessary for transformative learning" and advises "blocking out power relationships" that are known to get in the way of communications between teachers and learners (p. 31). However, he does not appear to give explanations nor examples of how to achieve this goal.

When Boyd (1991) says "primordial elements," he refers to both (a) elements in the small group that represent various archetypal figures in a group and also (b) those same elements as mirrored and operating inside each individual group member: "In the course of a group's life the social system expresses many different primordial patterns" such as the "Great Mother," the "Great Father," anima and animus, and the shadow among others" (p.

210). It appears that for Boyd, factors beyond simply the rational impact of the group on the individual are considerable in the dynamics of transformative learning.

In Boyd's (1991) approach, the group leader does not participate except when needed to mirror the dynamics among the primordial elements in the group, so as to facilitate group members more clearly seeing these elements, that is to raise the consciousness of members with timely metaphors (pp. 219-233). His pathway to transformative learning for persons in group settings clearly goes beyond the rational, cognitive reframing central for the autonomous learner in Mezirow's (1991, 2000) approach. In an overview of transformative learning approaches, we read: "Mezirow. . . focuses on cognitive conflicts experienced by the individual's relationship with culture, Boyd. . . on conflicts within the individual's psyche and the resolution among these entities that leads to a transformation" (Taylor, 1998, p. 3).

Typically, a Cooperative Inquiry is initiated by one or more people who have experienced a disturbing dilemma or some sort of wake-up call centered on a topic of personal interest (Bray, Lee, Smith, & Yorks, 2000, p. 52). The initiator then invites others to participate in a series of action/reflection cycles focused on the topic at hand. For Heron, the optimal power structure is for all participants to co-lead the processes of the group, differing from both Mezirow and Boyd in this regard.

7. CONTINUE TO EXPLORE THE WRITING DILEMMAS ON YOUR OWN JOURNEY

In significant ways, the above approaches to transformative learning seem similar. First, an initial "dilemma" is confronted by an adult human being as a central spark setting off a learning journey. In addition, each of these three approaches envisions an adult learner engaged in a process over time, deepened by a series of stages. Pain and discomfort are to be expected in each of the models of how transformative learning happens; they all seem to follow the wisdom of Kahlil Gibran: "Your pain is the breaking of the shell that encloses your understanding" (2002, p. 52). All approaches utilize the context of a group, and profound transformative shifts can result from participating such approaches.

8. STRIVE FOR BALANCE

"Research Cycling" is a way to try and ensure enough cycles of action and reflection by enough participants, so as to provide plenty of both positive and negative feedback on the inquiry topic. Feedback is essential to the operations of any system. Positive feedback shows members what areas should be pursued; negative shows which areas are "ungrounded, irrelevant, beside the point" (Heron, 1996, p. 131). In our group, we did express both positive and negative feedback during our group reflections, which let us identify areas to pursue and those to drop. For example, we realized we had been out on an irrelevant limb when we ventured into our focus on fear as a component of creating a story with conflict, as noted earlier.

Another validity measure is to work toward a "balance of divergence and convergence" in order to "articulate the research topic more [or less] thoroughly" (Heron, 1996, p. 60). Here, as in other validity aspects, it is expected that groups will vary in their balance of divergence and convergence. For the most part in our group, we converged by all going with the same action plan, yet we diverged by going with a variety of action strategies individually. For example, Bridget often used clustering (Rico, 1983) to get her stories started, while Kate interviewed friends and family, and Lilly meditated on the correspondence between the act of making love and the action of writing and forming a story.

Furthermore, the cycling between action and reflection needs to be "balanced" in order to draw on the multiple ways of knowing assumed by the Participatory Worldview (Heron, 1996, pp. 140-142). In order to avoid either too much action with slight reflection or its opposite, too much meaning based on too little experience, each inquiry group needs to agree on what a good balance is for its purposes, considering the practical demands of participants' other commitments.

WEBSITES

60+ Ways of Learning
https://quizlet.com/97294943/chapter-7-and-8-flash-cards/

California Institute of Integral Studies
https://www.ciis.edu

California Writers Club http://calwriters.org

Cooperative Inquiry
https://en.wikipedia.org/wiki/Cooperative_inquiry

June Gillam www.junegillam.com

Reason & Heron, Short Guide to CI
http://www.human-inquiry.com/cishortg.htm

William Torbert http://www.williamrtorbert.com

BIBLIOGRAPHY

Alvarez, J. (2000). Preface. In J. Sternburg (Ed.), *The writer on her work* (pp. xi-xviii). New York: W. W. Norton.

Barth, J. (1999). Incremental perturbation: How to know whether you've got a plot or not. In J. Checkoway (Ed.), *Creating fiction: Instruction and insights from teachers of the Associated Writing Programs* (pp. 126-134). Cincinnati, OH: Story Press.

Bell, M. S. (1997). *Narrative design: Working with imagination, craft, and form.* New York: W. W. Norton.

Bell, James Scott. (2012). Crafting Novels & Short Stories. Cincinnati, Ohio: Writer's Digest Books.

Boyd, R. D. (1991). Personal transformations in small groups: A Jungian perspective. New York: Routledge.

Bradbury, R. (1990). Zen in the art of writing: Releasing the creative genius within you. New York: Bantam Books.

Bray, J., Lee, J., Smith, L., & Yorks, L. (2000). *Collaborative inquiry in practice: Action, reflection, and meaning making.* Thousand Oaks, CA: Sage.

Browne, R., & King, D. (2004). Self-Editing for Fiction Writers (2nd ed.) New York: Harper Collins.

Burroway, J. (2000). Writing fiction: A guide to narrative craft (5th ed.). New York: Longman.

Cameron, J. (1996). *The vein of gold: The kingdom of story.* Boulder, CO: Sounds True.

DeSalvo, L. (1999). Writing as a way of healing: How telling our stories transforms our lives. San Francisco: HarperSanFrancisco.

Egri, L. (1960). The art of dramatic writing: Its basis in the creative interpretation of human motives. New York: Touchstone Books.

Estes, C. (1991). *The creative fire: Myths and stories about the cycles of creativity.* Boulder, CO: Sounds True.

Estes, C. (1992). Women who run with the wolves: Myths and stories of the wild woman archetype. New York: Ballantine Books.

Ferraiolo, Wm. (2017) Meditations on Self-Discipline and Failure: Stoic Exercise for Mental Fitness. Online: O-Books.

Fisher, D., & Torbert, W. (1995). Personal and organizational transformations: The true challenge of continual quality improvement. London: McGraw-Hill.

Frey, J. N. (2000). The key: How to write damn good fiction using the power of myth. New York: St. Martin's Press.
Gardner, H. (1993). *Multiple intelligences: The theory in practice.* New York: HarperCollins.

Gardner, J. (1991). *The art of fiction: Notes on craft for young writers.* New York: Vintage Books.

Gardner, J. (1999). On becoming a novelist. New York: W. W. Norton.

Gibran, K. (2002). *The prophet.* New York: Alfred A. Knopf. (Original work published in 1923)

Gillam, J. (2008). Creating Juicy Tales: Cooperative Inquiry into Writing Stories. Germany: Lambert Academic Publishing.

Goldberg, N. (1994). *Wild mind: Living the writer's life.* Austin, TX: Writer's AudioShop.

Gordon, M. (2000). The parable of the cave or: In praise of watercolors. In J. Sternburg (Ed.), *The writer on her work* (pp. 27-32). New York: W. W. Norton.

Heron, J. (1996). Cooperative inquiry: Research into the human condition. London: Sage.

Jong, E. (2000). Blood and guts: The tricky problem of being a woman writer in the late twentieth century. In J. Sternburg (Ed.), *The writer on her work* (pp. 169-179). New York: W. W. Norton.

Keen, S. (1990). *The power of stories workshop: Illuminating your life's meaning through stories.* Boulder, CO: Sounds True.

Kochman, T. (1981). *Black and white styles in conflict*. Chicago: The University of Chicago Press.

Lamott, A. (1994). Bird by bird: Some instructions on writing and life. New York: Pantheon Books.

Mezirow, J. (1991). *Transformative dimensions of adult learning*. San Francisco: Jossey-Bass.

Mezirow, J. (2000). Learning to think like an adult: Core concepts of transformation theory. In J. Mezirow & Associates, *Learning as transformation: Critical perspectives on a theory in progress* (pp. 3-33). San Francisco: Jossey-Bass.

Mezirow, J., & Associates. (2000). *Learning as transformation: Critical perspectives on a theory in progress*. San Francisco: Jossey-Bass.

Mindell, A. (1995). *Sitting in the fire: Large group transformation using conflict and diversity*. Portland, OR: Lao Tse Press.

Moore, T. H. (1964). *Henry Miller on writing*. New York: New Directions Paperbook.

Reason, P., & Heron, J. (1999). A layperson's guide to co-operative inquiry. Retrieved January 31, 1999, from University of Bath, Center for Action Research in Professional Practice Web site: http://www.bath.ac.uk/carpp/layguide.htm

Rico, G. (1983). *Writing the natural way: Using right-brain techniques to release your expressive powers.* Los Angeles: J. P. Tarcher.

Rico, G. (2000). Creating re-creations: Inspiration from the source. Spring, TX: Absey & Co.

Roediger, D. (Ed.). (1998). *Black on white: Black writers on what it means to be white.* New York: Schocken Books.

Saricks, J. G. (2009). The Readers' Advisory Guide to Genre Fiction (2nd ed.). Chicago: American Library Association.

Scott, S. (1997). Grieving as a dynamic process in transformation. In P. Armstrong, N. Miller, & M. Zukas (Eds.), *Crossing borders, breaking boundaries: Proceedings of the 27th Annual SCUTREA Conference.* (pp. 409-413). London: Standing Conference on University Teaching and Research in the Education of Adults.

Taylor, E. W. (1998). *The theory and practice of transformative learning: A critical review.* (Information Series No. 374). Columbus, OH: ERIC Clearinghouse on Adult, Career, & Vocational Education.

Torbert, W. (1991). The power of balance. Newbury Park, CA: Sage.

Welsh, C., & Gillam, J. (2000). Four-Color analysis: Applying Torbert's four territories in the classroom. In C. Wiessner, S. Meyer, & D. Fuller (Eds.), Proceedings of the third international conference on transformative learning. Challenges of practice: Transformative learning in action (pp. 47-49). New York: Columbia University Teachers College, Center for Educational Outreach & Innovation.

    Welsh, C.A. (2003). Four-color analysis of text: A pragmatic, constructivist, and integral approach to writing and comprehension of text (Doctoral dissertation). ProQuest Dissertation and Theses database. (UMI No 3093567)

    Woolf, V. (1929). *A room of one's own.* New York: Harcourt, Brace, & World.

Appendix A.

Ground Rules For Safety In The Group,
from the CREATING JUICY TALES List

1. Confidentiality
2. Spelling doesn't count
3. Ideas/opinions/writings can be criticized but not the person
4. We all have the right to pass or to reveal as much as we choose
5. Come on time or early to the meetings
6. Take care of/responsibility for our own needs
7. Agree to add to the rules as we go along

Writing in Small Groups the 4color Way

Appendix B. OUR ACTION PLANS AND STORIES

Writers in alpha order	1st STORY action plan: write a story containing conflict	2nd STORY action plan: write a story springing from seven meaning-ful concepts	3rd STORY action plan: write a story where a character experiences fear resulting in conflict	4th STORY action plan: write connections & disconnections with obstacles causing change
BRIDGET	poor mom denies daughter fashion top but buys cigarettes for herself	nice but classist teacher tries to control aide and student	woman overwhelmed by workload has panic attack over fear of not writing	teacher tries to teach students to manage emotions but lets her own go to violent extremes
ELEANOR	women clash at garden club meeting, one throws pot through greenhouse roof at end	two sisters play a game; older sister turns card table over at losing to younger one	daughter fears father will physically attack mother & tries to protect mother	Woman fears daughter will die, turns to religion that husband is strongly against
KATE	wife and new mother-in-	woman inquires of family	woman avoids worrying	husband has a son he's kept a secret

65

	law clash over holidays and ways to treat family	& friends, searching for conflicts to write about	over her own health and worries about others' health	from his wife
LILLY	"N.I.M.B.Y." neighbors in racial conflict; one of their houses burns down	rewrite of first story with clearer conflict, neighbors throw things back & forth	woman fears Email threats to bomb shopping malls, warns friends and family	Woman experiences increasing abuse goes from bad to worse
MARCELLA	woman searches to uncover lies told her during childhood	woman hides her spiritual heritage to fit in with gossipy community	boy fears Halloween but gets no help from insensitive adults	teacher preoccupied with cheating husband misses student's suicide clue
PETUNIA	woman tries to stay on yellow brick road to happiness, road shifts shape	a junkman wants a friend but does not know how to be a friend	no story-- absent this meeting	therapist deals with a client waving gun around during marriage counseling session

Writing in Small Groups the 4color Way

STAR				
	no story-- absent this meeting	woman both loves and hates her boyfriend's son	characters in coffee shop struggle against their roles amidst gossip	a play based around the coffee shop conflicts and gossip

June Gillam

Appendix C. (from the second story "Eleanor" wrote in the CI dissertation project)

MONOPOLY

By June Gillam

AFTER A QUICK LUNCH of bologna sandwiches, Mother pulled a plastic bag of See's samples from the cool depths of her purse. "Don't forget girls, no TV." Leaving them with the chocolate, a closet full of board games, and the echoes of her good sportsmanship slogans, Mother went back to work at See's candy store, her high heels clacking as she walked out the door.

"I'm teaching you Monopoly today, Billie." Margaret smiled brightly at her little sister and popped a See's sample into her mouth, chewing fast. She didn't care what kind it was, she loved them all, not just for the taste but for the way they made her feel. "Remember, even if you lose, you have to be a good sport, O.K.? Here, you carry the box outside."

Margaret needed to get the old card table out of the family room. She didn't want to be playing in the same room where Daddy had launched the table and everything else into this lonely new life. Stuffing her last two pieces of See's into her mouth, she fought the temptation to sneak one of Billie's out of the fridge where her little sister had already stashed it for later.

Muscular for nine, Margaret lugged the heavy table out into the long green backyard, edged with gnarly old plum trees. She yanked out each folded-up steel leg and snapped it into place, swinging the card table into position on the overgrown grass near the fence, lined with lush old peony bushes heavy with flowers, each blowzy white bloom crawling with ants. Margaret felt angry as she set up the Monopoly game, something to keep seven-year-old Billie busy on this awful day, the first afternoon of summer vacation when Margaret was in charge. Daddy was gone and Mother wasn't home anymore either, just the two of them in a silent house.

Margaret sent Billie back inside to get another folding chair. Adjusting her own chair in a spot on the lawn where sunlight filtered through the blackish plum tree branches, Margaret took off her tortoise shell glasses and gazed into the fluffy white peonies next to the table. They reminded her of the huge white popcorn balls Mother made for trick or treat last year. Margaret was amazed at

how the blooms opened themselves and allowed ants full run of their feathery petals. Tracking the same path, up and down the peony stalks bursting with buds, up and down the nearby plum tree trunks oozing with sap, ants busied themselves endlessly, gathering sticky sweets to nourish the life underfoot, under control of their queen.

She rubbed her palms across her cheeks, growing hot with the memory of Adelaide and Char after they found her in the girls' bathroom, the day after Daddy moved out last April. Her thick lenses were streaked from tears and Margaret was trying to dry them with paper towels. All she was getting was a smeary mess, when Addy and Char came bursting in through the swinging doors and started taunting her with "four-eyed, freckle face, red head" in a sing song chant. Margaret's lazy eye turned in as she stared at them in shock, and they started yelling that she was crazy and running out of the bathroom like they were scared of her.

Still, Margaret was stunned to get home after school that day and find a hand-scrawled "wanted" poster thumb tacked to her front door: "Wanted—Margaret Kovar—Just Escaped From the Nut House!" None of the neighborhood stay-at-home moms would let their kids come play with Billie anymore either, since Mother had gone to work. Picky Mrs. Barnes even took Susan out of Billie's tap dance class. The two sisters were stuck with each other all summer, for better or worse.

Margaret rubbed her eyes and turned back to the card table—those ants touching antennae as they met on their trails would not go for that kind of torturing their own.

Placing the colored Monopoly money in neat stacks, Margaret explained the rules of the game as Little Billie's piercing chocolate brown eyes watched her set up the board, the bank, the Chance and Community Chest cards. Billie picked the top hat for her game piece while Margaret chose her favorite, the flat iron. Peering through her thick lenses, she brushed off a scout ant that had managed to find its way over to her goldenrod five hundred dollar bills while Billie squealed in terror over the ant.

The game wound on through the afternoon, as sun poured over them in mottled patterns through the plum branches. Billie kept alert for any sign of ants on the table, but Margaret relaxed into a feeling that everything was under control now. Daddy had taught her to play Monopoly one night a couple years ago, letting her sit on his lap and move his tiny aluminum race car around the board. She always loved staying up late with the grown-ups.

Glare from the game board reflected off the young girls' faces in the California Valley heat as they shook dice and chased each other's aluminum playing pieces around the board.

Billie was catching on well for seven. Gradually, she began to buy up more valuable property than Margaret, who could taste bologna burps from the rushed lunch with Mother. They used to get BLTs, her favorite, but Mother didn't have time for those now. She wished she had more See's candy to soothe the stomach ache she was getting watching Billie stack up high-end property deeds.

"Give me Park Place," shouted Billie, tapping her tiny aluminum top hat on the luxury property.

"You could say 'Please.'" Playing a dual role of banker and etiquette coach, Margaret jiggled the card table, steadying the steel legs into the warm earth beneath.

"Park Place—please!" Billie squealed, thrusting three pieces of Monopoly money towards the bank. Margaret glared through her thick lenses at her little sister.

It was just like last March, when Billie waved her See's rocky road Easter egg past Margaret's pale blue eyes. They both started out the same, hoarding basket candy in shoeboxes, visions of sugar fixes dancing in their daydreams. But Margaret—who should have known better, who was the most grown up, who hated herself for her weakness—Margaret tore open the Adidas box she'd Scotch-taped shut to guard against her greedy nature. She ripped the lid off and devoured chocolate eggs, marshmallow chicks, and jellybeans hiding in shreds of plastic grass. Despite her good intention, by the day after Easter, Margaret's shoebox was empty, a rectangle of darkness, void.

Over the next few weeks Billie took teensy, ant-size bites of her See's egg, in the face of her poverty-stricken sister.

Sucking in the corners of her lips and wishing she'd saved her after- lunch chocolate samples for now, Margaret reached across the table, yanked the money from Billie's grasp, and sorted it into slots in the Monopoly bank. The singsong rhythms of Mother's "it's how you play the game" mantra echoed through Margaret's cells. The sportsmanship slogans came at them daily, since Daddy's temper erupted on that worst night ever. Mother had gone to see Pagliacci with Aunt May, leaving Daddy home with the girls. Daddy called up Uncle Warren and Uncle Lester for poker while the women were "out on the town" as Daddy called going to the opera.

Margaret loved it when Daddy's brothers came to visit, especially when Mother was gone. The men let them stay up late and watch quietly till they got sleepy. The vigor of the poker games, laced with the spicy smells of Jack Daniel's and big fat cigars, flooded Margaret with conviction that all was right with the world. Even later as she lay in the bedroom she shared with Billie and drifted to dreamland, Margaret felt soothed by the hearty laughter out in the family room.

It was hard for her to sort out what really happened that night though, from the nightmare it blurred into later. As if in a dream, she heard cursing, crashing and slamming. Fueled by whiskey and the hot slapping of cards onto the table, the clatter of plastic chips scraping across the table top, the three brothers reverted to their rough Minnesota youth, arguing over who used to bag more ducks in the dawn light, who used to nail that first buck in the fall. Competitive blood pounding, their laughter heated up and burst into flames of curse words and fists crashing on the old card table set up in the family room.

    Daddy was the oldest of the three brothers, the one who came out to California and started the painting business that gave them all jobs. Daddy was the one who was always the winner. He didn't know how to lose.

    What Margaret remembered for certain was lying wide-eyed and petrified in bed until she heard Daddy's ragged snoring from her parents' bedroom. She crept out to the darkened family room. By the slim light of a new moon streaming in the windows, a blurry chaos spread itself before her dim vision, the leftovers of a night when nobody won. Kings, Queens, and Jacks alongside other cards lay flung onto every square foot of the forest green carpet. The card table was over on its side, one leg folded at a crazy angle, highball glasses lay near puddles of whiskey-tinged melting ice, the ashtray split into ceramic shards, ashes dusted the scene.

    Margaret stood in her blue flannel nightgown, frozen. Silently so as not to wake Daddy or Little Billie, Margaret picked up each scrap of the mess. Her heart felt heavy as wet clay. Mother just wouldn't understand a poker game ending like that. Finally, numb as if she had never awakened, Margaret crawled underneath her covers and fell back into sleep.

June Gillam

Next morning, Mother discovered the broken ashtray in the trash, which led to her piecing together the whole story. Then she started up with the sportsmanship slogans, sprinkled over Daddy, brothers-in-law, daughters and anyone who came into her range. Aunt May bolstered Mother's cause, holding forth in a thin reedy voice her view that each person has an inner seed atom, setting them in motion. A bad inner core drives nasty tempers, poor sportsmanship, and violence in the home. Nothing can change that fact, May would declare, pursing her thin lips into a tidy rosette, and staring at each person's torso as if she could perceive the quality of the seed atom pulsating there.

After the poker party disaster, Aunt May told Mother she was lucky that Margaret took after their side of the family, calm and collected, under control. No one mentioned competitive Little Billie, the one named after her Daddy Bill.

Most shocking to Margaret, Daddy and Mother started arguing more than ever before. Daddy yelled and Mother was quiet, but mad. Daddy was throwing things, too, after he thought the girls were asleep. Soon Daddy was sleeping out on the family room sofa, and by the end of April, he was gone. Aunt May said it was good riddance. Mother tried to get child support, help with the yard work, or just anything from Daddy, but he had vanished from town. As summer vacation began, Mother had to go to work, leaving the two girls with orders for no television because she thought it was a bad influence. Mother figured Margaret was old enough at nine to watch her sister.

Writing in Small Groups the 4color Way

Glaring down at her apt little Monopoly pupil, Margaret passed over the cardboard Park Place deed, with its crisp royal blue header. Billie stacked it on top of the five other prime properties she'd purchased in the several hours since the lesson began.

"Now," Billie flashed her bright-eyed, gap-toothed grin, "I'll take four houses, please." Withdrawing creamy hundred-dollar bills from her many-colored stash tucked under her game board edge, Billie waved play money out over the board, her little pink tongue resting between the four-tooth gap in her top front teeth.

Margaret began to feel the gnawing inside she'd felt when Billie pulled from her Capezio shoebox that glossy, untouched See's rocky road egg a week after Easter. It was still as shiny as the black patent tap shoes Billie loved so much.

Snatching her little sister's play money, Margaret tossed it unsorted into the bank, and flung four tiny green houses across the table in Billie's direction, one of which fell onto the long green lawn, unmowed since Daddy was gone.

Grinning, Billie pinched two houses side by side and fit them onto her dark blue Park Place border. She positioned a third on her blue Boardwalk property, then jumped off her folding chair, to kneel down and flick through spikes of long grass, searching for her fourth house.

Margaret bent low to observe the real estate hunt, fantasizing the tiny green house and Billie melting together like nutty rocky road into the hot grassy dirt, tunneled with ants. Margaret smiled at her secret image of Billie wedged in the ant tunnels.

June Gillam

Billie spotted her lost house lying among the long green blades, grasped it between her small fingers, sat up straight-backed, and nudged it into the Boardwalk border. Her brown eyes zigzagged between her high-end game-board empire and Margaret's aluminum flat iron Monopoly piece, sitting safely on Community Chest, headed directly toward the new green houses on Park Place and Boardwalk. "Your turn!" Billie sang out in a loud thin voice.

Praying for a two or a three. Even a five or seven. Not a four or six. Not four, not six, Margaret rubbed the dice back and forth nine times to match her age, relishing the clacking sounds, then flung them toward the scraped-up edges of the old table, the same one where Daddy used to beat his brothers at poker back when he still lived at home, time after time, in his Jack Daniel's jubilation, until that night when losers took all.

Margaret clutched at her ears as each die came to rest. Echoes from Mother rang in her mind: It doesn't matter if you win or lose, it doesn't matter! She adjusted her tortoise shell glasses and stared through the thick lenses at the two ivory cubes, glaring so bright in the sun that she couldn't add up the sum of their spots.

"Threes!" Billie sang out. "You've got two threes, that's six! That'll be six hundred dollars rent!" She sat back and crossed her legs, lady-like in her folding chair. "Please."

Margaret's stomach felt rocky with buried walnut halves and marshmallows, coated in bitter chocolate. She sat in the dappled sunshine, burning with a frozen heat. Carefully then, she counted out the few bills still lodged under her player's edge of the game board: "One...two...fifty...seventy five..." Trying to be the best

Writing in Small Groups the 4color Way

sport she could, Margaret handed over every piece of her paper money to her little sister.

"Sorry, that's not six hundred!" In the glare of the hot June sun, Billie's gap-toothed gums glistened pink. "I win! I win!" She jumped off her old folding chair and ran around in the back yard, clicking her soles on the concrete sidewalk bisecting the long green grass, parallel to the row of plum trees and peony bushes.

Margaret stared at her loss, spread out in plain view across the tabletop, her stomach radiating energy from that spot Aunt May said was her seed atom.

Her arms stretched out in the heat, and she watched her own fiery fingers clamp over the worn edges of the old tan card table. She lifted it up easily, Monopoly board and all, up off the long green lawn, shocked by its lightness, oblivious of her own strength, and heaved it straight up into the hot summer air, up and over in the direction Billie was tap dancing. Higher and higher—past the plum tree branches it rose—then hung in the sky like a snapshot. Tiny green houses, red hotels, pink, gold, and turquoise money, cardboard property deeds, and aluminum playing pieces poured down, to vanish from view among the long grass of summer into a tiny ant-tunneled world.

Margaret ran into the house, not looking back.

--A 2700-word short story first published in *Metal Scratches*, Issue 5, 2005, under the byline J. E. Gillam.
©June Gillam

June Gillam

Appendix D.

MY DISORIENTING DILEMMA
Why go to all this trouble to learn to write stories?

In July 1990, I enrolled for a summer class at University of California, Davis, as a way to improve my skills teaching English at a California Community College. The intensive two-week Writing Project invited teachers to more fully inhabit both sides of the desk; it encouraged us not only to require writing from students but also to write along with them.

Our instructor told us a detailed story from her childhood in which she had hid out on a sloping rooftop as a private place to escape her family and live in her daydreams. She told us this long story to demonstrate the teacher doing what she was about to ask us to do. She put us in small groups to share out loud what she called "stories told regularly at family gatherings," so we could practice this oral method of pre-writing.

Although usually an energetic participant in writing classes, I found myself tongue tied at this supposedly simple exercise. I had had plenty of experience with college papers and with poetry, but had written virtually no stories. I managed to recount a brief vignette about my youngest sister and a time I had been sent out in the neighborhood to find her. But I wasn't worried that she might be in danger and there was no tension in my story, so no one in my small group seemed engaged. Although the other teachers kindly asked questions to elicit details to make the story more exciting, when I went home and phoned my sisters, they did not know specifics about what happened either. I felt humiliated that I had no interesting family stories, which seemed to be something that most folks were expected to have, including the teachers in the Area III Writing Project and, by extension, their students.

This "failure" was a heartfelt turning point, a moment of disquiet, a disorienting dilemma. I began to explore my problem in a short piece I titled "Storyteller":

Storyteller never came to live at our house. Oh, she used to visit us now and then as she prowled the neighborhood, and we welcomed her. After we clustered in close, she would begin to glitter and gesture and jingle and jangle while we raptly listened and laughed. But she didn't really fit in with us because of the talons at the tips of her lively fingers. Although her talons generally just left faint red streaks on the main characters, sometimes they drew a bit of blood.

Even though our own characters would probably have healed up quickly, we were too tender to risk even minor woundings at her hands. Our Grandma had taught us not to say anything at all if we couldn't say something nice, and we were very obedient, so we earnestly worked at weaving our words to build our characters up.

But on quiet evenings, we could hear streams of laughter coming from the neighbors across the street, who had been able to adopt Storyteller. We listened, and we wondered if we could toughen up and ask her to visit again (Kraemer, 1990, p. 34).

June Gillam

The UC Davis instructor "published" our class writings in a booklet as an example of ways to validate and motivate students. In her introductory note to the informal publication, she claimed the value of stories as ways of knowing, and ended by assuring readers that Storyteller is indeed present among us:

Interesting to ponder the fact that for so long, the teaching of writing seemed to presume that anything personal should be reserved for personal diaries or "Creative Writing" courses at best. Clearly, it seemed, these were not the source of true insight. That could only be gotten from books and objectivity.

Likewise, writing was expected to take on the guise of TRUTH through exposition; narrative was thought to be frivolous, the idle efforts of the artists and the storytellers.

In the pages that follow, TRUTH is shown, not told . . . and it's told in the personal stories and family stories of a group of people who, two weeks ago, were complete strangers to one another. Through these writings, we are strangers no more, and life seems just a bit more comprehensible.

Enjoy these, June (and everyone else) . . . the Storyteller is among us (Kraemer, 1990, p. ii).

That U.C. Davis summer school class popped opened my eyes to my difficulty in writing story, and the next year I enrolled in another writing class at U.C. Davis. Although energetically producing journals and poems, I struggled mightily with story and especially began to battle against the explicit requirement for conflict in story, as the teacher claimed was necessary.

Writing in Small Groups the 4color Way

Why, I wondered. Why did there have to be conflict in stories? The first part of my problem was that somehow I could not accept that there had to be conflict in stories, now that I was on the creating "side" of them rather than the reading and literary analysis side. In order to assist us in freeing our writer-voices, the U.C. Davis instructor led us into objectifying our inner critics, using expressive art materials. After a long period of silent work in the classroom, my own mother at her most witchy leered back at me from my drawing of her--my critic, most specifically in writing prose narrative: a life-like antagonist. With a shock, I realized that I had no clue how to write a dramatic story with a villain and that for me, writing people in conflict was off limits.

Mother

As I continued to explore this problem over the next ten years, I came to see that I was somehow raised "story-deprived." My deeply religious Christian Science mother taught my sisters and me that if we couldn't say something nice, not to say anything at all. I had been raised to stay out of trouble or at least not to talk about it, whereas the late novelist and writing teacher John Gardner (1999) says that dramatic story requires people "getting themselves into trouble" (p. 122). I can remember being cautioned by Mom not to gossip, that it was not true, kind, that it was petty, that we were expected to be "above" telling stories about people. Mom read us lyrical and inspirational poetry and we discussed moral and ethical ideas--we read the King James Bible and Mary Baker Eddy's Science and Health with Key to the Scriptures from an early age. However, we did not read the Bible for its stories, but rather through the lens of conceptual abstractions Mrs. Eddy had written as the "key" to the scriptures. Although there was plenty of literacy, ideas, and love of learning, there was no family story in our house, no emphasis on human beings in actual action--for the most part, no one told or listened to stories.

Our Grandma Frosia counseled our mother that "children should be seen and not heard." When Mom passed this along to us, I can recall feeling shocked into silence. One of my most vivid memories of Grandma Frosia is of her triplet brass monkeys posed in the famous "see no evil, hear no evil, speak no evil" postures. The odd thing was that although no one in the family verbalized what the message was, the minute my eyes spotted the brass figure on Grandma Frosia's knick-knack shelf, I understood the meaning from the postures of the three monkeys. A major value in my upbringing, this triple prohibition kept conflict, among other evils such as even talking about conflict, swept into the very back corners of our family closet.

As part of my English master's degree program, I had taken a "Grandmother, Mother, and Me" class and interviewed my great aunt about her sister, my maternal grandmother, who bore and raised seven children. Though Aunt May told mostly factual description or sunny tales, I got hints of the struggles in Grandma Frosia's life. However, giving out the details of Frosia's repeatedly taking her growing number of children and running away from what I later learned was her abusive, alcoholic husband, our Grandpa Tom, was "too dreary" for Aunt May. I didn't press her, since this was not our family's way and I was not then aware of how silenced around story we were. At the end of our interview, I asked: "Did [Grandma Frosia] ever wish that she had done something else besides get married and have all those children?"

"I doubt it," said Aunt May, "she never talked about it, if she did. We used to sit and talk over all these times we went through together--and she always wanted to write the story of her life." This line haunts me now; it seems tragic that my grandmother wanted to write the story of her life, yet she never did. I wrote the surface of her life for her by way of my interview with her sister, Aunt May, several years after Frosia had been silenced by a stroke. I was so unaware of the value of story, though, that I did not even share with my siblings the resulting 20-page biography of our grandmother's life as told by her sister until about 18 years after I wrote it, after Frosia, May, and our mother Geraldine were all dead.

Father

It was not just Mother's family who posted the "No conflict" sign in my writer's garden; my handsome, gregarious father was part of the process, as well. In an essay in The Writer on Her Work, Mary Gordon (2000) asks: "Where did I acquire my genius for obedience? I had a charming father. . . . [to whom I brought] great joy, and I learned the pleasures of being a good girl" (p. 31). My painting contractor father would take me, all dolled up like Shirley Temple by my housewife mom, around town with him, to brighten the lives of his business associates during the anxious years of World War II. I was trained early to avoid taking on what writer Honor Moore (2000) calls the "conflict between art and female obligation" (p. 47). When I was a bit grouchy, in a mood to quarrel, Daddy would tease me out of it and seal his case with lines such as "You can catch more flies with honey than you can with vinegar." I can relate to Gordon when she writes: "I did not have the courage for clear rage. There is no seduction like that of being thought a good girl" (p. 28). I was raised to become and to remain "happiness bringer," as one of my very close women friends named me decades later.

Middle-Class White Culture

Not only my parents, but also the middle-class white American culture of the last half of the 20th century ironed me into a conflict-avoiding, flat line type of writer. Canadian educator Sue Scott (1997) calls ours a "be happy, 'positive thinking' cultural reality" (p. 412), one in which pain and other difficulties are often discounted. Arnold Mindell (1995) writes that "the mainstream in every country tends to skirt the anger of the oppressed classes.... Western thought is biased toward peace and harmony" (p. 36). An incident in a high school physical education class in the late 1950's illustrates this cultural filter in my own experience.

Our all-white girls' basketball team one day beat an all-black girls' team. In 1957, we were ignorant of racial issues in our lives and at school; I don't recall seeing blacks in school except in gym class and don't recall ever playing an all black team before or after this incident. My friend Judy and I were co-captains of our team but thought nothing of this gym-class victory and afterwards went about our teenage business. That evening, Judy and I each got a phone call at home, threatening us about having won the game; we did not take these threats seriously, though, not having had experience with being victims.

The next day, as I walked out of history class, one of the black basketball players pressed up close to me, clamping her arm around my waist and steering me over to the side of the hall and on into the girls' bathroom; I was yelling for help loudly the whole way. As she was pushing me up against one of the bathroom sinks, another black girl from the team stepped out of a bathroom stall, and pressed up to me as well; I kept yelling and a young white male teacher came running in and rescued me. He escorted both black girls to the principal's office; I was not even called into the principal's office. Judy and I found out later that the girls were suspended for some time.

My friends and I were so unaware of conflict that we basically forgot about this incident and were not troubled by the black girls again. I guess it was a sort of safe and in some ways charmed white middle class life, but not without its own hidden costs, one of which was my own ordeal in trying to learn to explicitly value, create, and imagine conflict in writing stories. I had lived a privileged white life, including the unearned luxury of not having to struggle for my rights every day, but was becoming struck by the cost to me as a writer of this so-called privilege, part of the cost of deep-rooted racism in my culture.

In Black and White Styles in Conflict, Thomas Kochman (1981) says "white culture compels individuals to internalize and repress anger" (p. 125), adding that blacks see whites as "interpersonally weak" (p. 126). Looking back, I can see that my high school friends and I kept ourselves silenced and insulated in a white cocoon;

we "wound the circle of [our] experiences . . . more and more tightly" and chose to "opt for safety instead of life" as the white historian David Roediger (1998) writes, quoting James Baldwin (p. 22). In her Preface to The Writer on Her Work, Julia Alvarez (2000) asserts that women of her generation: "Need a new set of stories and voices in our heads to replace the shushing ones that had come to us from our culture, our books, our fathers, and, yes, our mothers too" (p. xii). This dissertation report is the story of creating a new set of stories and voices, beginning to push free, out past the tight circle of "shushing" forces.

Trying to Learn to Write Stories with Conflict

As mentioned above, two U. C. Davis writing classes in the early 1990s forced me to face the disorienting dilemma of my failure to write stories with engaging conflict. I continued to struggle with this problem because I love writing and had harbored the fantasy of writing a novel; it was a huge shock to have learned that I was unable to create a most basic element of a story: conflict. Therefore, I searched for ways to transform my writer self. I was teaching college composition, and when the instructor who had been teaching Creative Writing--Short Story announced her retirement, I asked to teach that class. I thought I would test the old saying that you learn best what you teach others, which in many ways had proved true for me earlier in tutoring and teaching composition as a graduate assistant at California State Sacramento.

My situation was in a way ironic, that an English teacher at a California Community College, who taught

Writing in Small Groups the 4color Way

writing, would find writing stories with conflict so extremely challenging. My situation confirmed what a colleague of mine who teaches public speaking claims: We all teach what we most need to learn. As part of my research to improve my knowledge and skills, I explored many "how to" write fiction books, searching for the way as much for myself as for my students. Teaching creative writing led to years of "learning about" how to write stories, including listening to audiotapes such as Sam Keen's (1990) The Power of Story Workshop and similar ones by Natalie Goldberg (1994), Clarissa Pinkola Estes (1991), and Julia Cameron (1996). Books such as Henry Miller on Writing (Moore, 1964) and many others full of advice on how to write story followed each other in rapid succession.

I was frank with my students and explained that I too was a student along with them, though I was by then in an advanced creative writing workshop which later turned into a writing support group. In spring of 1997, I did get a very short story published in an obscure outlet titled *Hodge Podge*, but the editor described it as a "multi-layered" piece, and it was as much poetic meditation as story. On behalf of my students and myself, I made connections with editors of magazines for writers and sent a couple of my own stories off to them for critique. I got the same response to my writing--lots of evocative description and hints at conflict but it was not clear enough to hold the readers' attention. On the other hand, one of my student's stories was published in one of those magazines, and he credited me with helping him on the story! I felt like a proverbial bridesmaid still yearning to be a bride, so to speak.

June Gillam

CIIS Transformative Learning and Change Program.

By the mid-nineties, I had heard of the Transformative Learning and Change doctoral program at California Institute of Integral Studies, and was delighted to learn that their curriculum honored story as a way of knowing, in addition to other ways. I was happy to be accepted into the program, in which we did write many of our papers in a sort of reflective narrative style. These papers were not necessarily meant to be stories containing conflict, although in recounting an important real-life critical incident as part of exploring transformative learning, I began to uncover and write out a bit of conflict based on my life's experiences. During this time, I also took some writing workshops and electives which were rich and informative but in which, again, I did not develop the skill of writing clear conflict, though I did make a few more steps towards this goal.

Exploring Why Stories Need Conflict

Not only could I not write conflict, I still did not understand why conflict must be present in order to have an engaging story. However, I kept searching with a gut feeling that knowing why might help me understand how.

I learned that most people who read stories keep turning the pages because some kind of instability, tension, or conflict in the narrative pulls them through-- they want to find out what happens next. Readers become bored when there is no conflict, says playwright and famous writing instructor Lajos Egri (1960), and most other theorists on writing dramatic narrative agree. "Conflict is the first encountered and the fundamental element of fiction. . . because in literature only trouble is interesting," writes Janet Burroway (2000), author of five editions of Writing Fiction, going on to quote Charles Baxter in Burning down the House: "Hell is story friendly. If you want a compelling story, put your protagonist among the damned. . . . Paradise. . . happens when the stories are over" (p. 29).

Egri (1960) wants writers to see how the "forces" in a story are "lined up" against each other, explaining that "forces may be groups, as well as individuals; Fascism vs. democracy, freedom vs. slavery" (p. 115). Characters in dramatic conflict at some level apparently value even their conflict: Egri (1960) notes the phrase "unity of opposites" means that characters are united in their fight; their "deep rooted" values and beliefs don't let them walk away from engagement in their conflict (p. 119).

Burroway (2000) briefly alludes to recent views that conflict is only partial to story, that conflict is "patriarchal," and that it might well be amended by less war-like metaphors of "connection and disconnection" (p. 33) to describe the dynamics of fiction. In this dissertation study, we would come to find ourselves deeply attending to various definitions of "conflict," as will be described later. However, in her 5th edition of Writing Fiction, Burroway (2000) remains aligned with the notion of conflict's central place in fiction, as we did, too, in this study.

Well-known writer and writing instructor John Gardner (1991) also supports the key role of conflict in plotting traditional dramatic fiction; in The Art of Fiction, he displays what he calls the "Fichtean curve" (p.

187). Gardner's geometric form is similar to the isosceles triangle shape of the Freitag triangle, which looks like a pyramid, from the traditional Aristotelian approach to plot (Bell, 1997, p. 27). Gardner (1991) notes that a protagonist in a dramatic narrative takes the difficult uphill line "b" slope of struggle and conflict to reach a desired goal instead of the flat, safe line "a" path of a boring character who moves along the baseline of the triangle where no danger lurks.

It is common to find the triangle form used to lay out the structure of conflict in traditional stories, with the protagonist fighting an uphill battle to reach his or her goal (Barth, 1999; Bell, 1997; Gardner 1991). These triangles look like a pointed mountain peak, with a horizontal baseline. Through my readings, I gradually came to realize that the role of conflict in a story is to give the characters a chance to face and try to climb the "mountain" of their antagonist, so to speak, to make choices, to learn and to grow. This journey seems similar to the process of transformative learning and change itself, which will be explored further in the final chapter of this dissertation report.

Problem Statement

The problem at the heart of initiating this dissertation study was my inadequate ability to create stories that contain dramatic tension or conflict. In addition, this lack of skill can be a problem for other writers who've had feedback from editors, support group peers, and teachers who ask, "Where is the conflict here?" Such writers, myself among them, have then struggled to locate or create conflict or tension in their stories. Certainly, people have various reasons for being unable to create dramatic narrative tension. I have described the context of my own experience, raised in a home where I was taught to be "a lady," to avoid overt conflict and awareness of it, as well. My own sense of disquiet arose in me due to being raised a "Goodie Two Shoes," taught to avoid conflict, taught that if I could not say something nice, not to say anything at all. Erica Jong (2000) writes, "I do not know what a writer would write about if all her characters were superwomen, cleansed of conflict. Conflict is the soul of literature" (p. 175).

I had seen this problem of being unable to create dramatic conflict among my students writing both fiction and non-fiction stories and among friends and acquaintances in writing support groups, too. It was clear that I was not alone, whatever the reasons for the difficulty. Although I had tried some traditional methods, I had still not learned the craft and continued to ask why I could not write stories with conflict in them.

Researcher's Assumptions

Some people believe that writers are born not made; however, I assumed writers can improve their craft, that it is possible to learn and change writing approaches, practices and outcome. I had become convinced that conflict in narrative is essential to creating stories that engage readers, and I assumed that learning to write such stories is valuable as a means of personal expression and communication. Further, I assumed that what could be learned from the process of writing dramatic stories including conflict might be valuable in many personal ways. I assumed that my ignorance of and inability to recognize, feel, and write conflict prevented me from experiencing the full range of human experience. In addition, I had a hunch that people may face common difficulties in writing conflict, but I did not assume their difficulties were caused by challenges similar to my own. Finally, I assumed that humans are life-long learners and can improve their practices at any age.

Researcher's Approach to Methodology

There are various approaches to learning how to improve one's craft as a writer some of which I had already tried as noted above, some solitary, some more sociable, some democratic, some authoritative. A woman might search for a suitable garret, romantic or otherwise, and take up residence, writing until finding one's way, pretty much as Virginia Woolf (1929) implies; if one has a room of one's own and the desire to write, then the writing should come. Woolf was my "shero," my role model; I hung a large photo print of her in my writing room as motivation. Unfortunately though, closeting myself in my writing room did not lead me to reaching my goal of writing conflict into stories.

Another way, as noted above, I tried to become a better story writer was to consult the vast array of self-help items such as books by Ray Bradbury (1990) and Anne Lamott (1994) and including audiotapes like Julia Cameron's (1996) Vein of Gold. In addition to taking in-person writing workshops and courses and joining writing support groups, I tried a correspondence course from the University of Iowa. While helpful in various ways, these methods alone did not help in achieving my goal of learning to write conflict in stories, although some of the time I did not yet have a clear picture of this goal.

Writing in Small Groups the 4color Way

Some important considerations in choosing methods to learn writing skills are the degree to which a person is alone and the degree to which feedback and input from others is involved--the social factor, which could also be termed the Inter/Intra-personal intelligence continuum in Howard Gardner's (1993) multiple intelligences or the Extrovert/introvert preferred styles going by Jungian temperament typologies (Thompson, 1996). Another factor of importance is the power differential that may exist, as in the case of a class with an autocratic teacher or a workshop with a possibly arrogant established writer. Related to the power differential is a significant third factor: the amount of risk-taking welcomed not only in the actual writing but also in the group dynamics.

As an extrovert and a kinesthetic learner, it was important for me to be physically with a group of writers. I can remember being envious of my husband, a writer for the Sacramento Bureau of the L. A. Times; whenever the reporters got stuck in writing an article or story, they could just get up, walk around and talk to the other reporters in the bureau. In many ways, I did not have the stereotypical introverted personality type to be a writer of stories, yet that desire had developed into a burning passion in my heart and soul. I sensed that writing story was a way to see more fully who I really was down under my lady-like exterior, and I instinctively looked for ways to improve my story writing inside a group setting.

Although we had focused on poetry fairly exclusively, the Feminist Writers' Guild (FWG) of years before had been terrific support for writing poetry: we self-published and performed our work at many local venues. But, by the time I realized I wanted and needed to learn to write stories, the FWG had disbanded. We did not have the organizational skills needed to keep the group alive, sorry to say. It was beginning to dawn on me that in order to have an effective learning support group, I needed to understand more about how to help sustain healthy groups.

Later, another group surfaced in Sacramento, a "cluster" of the International Women's Writing Group (IWWG), of which I became a charter member, with the hopes that we could surface and work though problems in the group so as to support its health and longevity. However, when faced with some interpersonal challenges among members, a majority of the group chose not to deal with them, preferring to stay on the "sunny" side, and assume that everyone was a "lady," as one member of the Sacramento cluster put it.

By this time, as part of the CIIS Transformative Learning and Change program, I had participated in one Cooperative Inquiry on the general topic of writing plus later, a year-long Cooperative Inquiry on the topic of white consciousness. These experiences felt like seeds planted that would later bloom into this dissertation study. I liked the way Cooperative Inquiry encourages full expression of emotions and values, including those that may be at odds with others' in the group. Because of these transformative learning experiences and my alignment with the Participative Worldview, I chose to use Cooperative Inquiry as the methodology to continue my research into how to write stories that included engaging conflict. I wanted to inquire into the problem of not being able to write stories containing conflict along with others who were interested in researching their own practice, rather than studying about writers, interviewing writers, or studying alone as a writer. I preferred to work in community, and so chose the Cooperative Inquiry methodology as a vehicle for transformative learning and change.

Due to the above-mentioned Cooperative Inquiry small groups having had only women in them, to my college literature courses having had a focus on women authors, and to my feeling most supported when working with women writers, I chose to focus this dissertation project on women inquiring into the topic of writing stories containing conflict.

Initial Research Question

Initially, my research question was simply "Can the craft of women writing dramatic narrative containing conflict be improved through the process of Cooperative Inquiry?" In Cooperative Inquiry, because the group participants are equal co-researchers and co-subjects, I had no more specific research question as such until my Cooperative Inquiry group met and we co-created our series of inquiry questions. I did, however, have a "Topic" to invite women to inquire into together: "Writing Stories Containing Conflict." Because of the Cooperative Inquiry methodology I planned to use, the group of women who chose to commit to this project shared the decisions about our research question, its formation and evolution, and what actions to take to begin to actively respond to the research question, to "test" it out, so to speak. These questions and action plans will be described in detail later. So, although my personal agenda energized my initiation of this inquiry, it did not direct the Cooperative Inquiry research after the initiation and orientation stage, as I hope is made clear in the body of this dissertation report.

Purpose
My purpose for this study was a blend of internal and external work from my perspectives as a struggling writer, a life-long learner, and a writing instructor. Initially, my purpose was to overcome my difficulty in creating narrative conflict for my own personal development as a writer and as a human being. Secondly, I wanted to see if Cooperative Inquiry could improve the practical skills of a group of writers to create conflict in stories. My final purpose was to learn from my experience of this cooperative research with the aim of using it as a possible pedagogy in the community college writing classes I teach.

I wanted to explore the process of my "nice" lady-like, white female self as she tried to become a crafter of stories containing conflict, trying to learn more deeply about my own human nature not from reading other authors' stories but by digging up my own buried stories and imagined stories. I wanted to experience what I suspected was the deeply educational value of the struggle to write conflict into story, as opposed to the well-respected value in academia of learning from reading about the conflict among characters in stories written by others. However, I was afraid to go on this important journey alone and felt a strong need for companions along the trail.

I wanted to see if the Cooperative Inquiry process could change my writer self and my co-researchers' writer selves into having the knack of writing improved dramatic narrative through a transformative type of

Writing in Small Groups the 4color Way

Cooperative Inquiry focused on the practical skills and craft of writing dramatic stories (Heron, 1996, p. 48). When I say "transform," I mean specifically changing from being unable to write conflict in stories to becoming able to do so by way of the transformative epistemology of Cooperative Inquiry's fourfold way of knowing. In other words, my focus was on learning how through the vehicle of fourfold way of knowing offered in Cooperative Inquiry, culminating in action more so than learning about theory alone.

    I was not looking for "truth" but for effectiveness in the craft of creating dramatic stories, a practical skill. I was not expecting to generalize results from this study onto other groups of writers nor to predict or control what might happen for other writers who read the dissertation report of this project. I was hoping we could teach ourselves the knack of writing dramatic narrative by the Cooperative Inquiry methodology, but I was not sure how this holistic process might enable us to achieve this goal. Whether our skills did or did not improve, I assumed we all would nevertheless have learned about ourselves as writers, as group members, and as learners.

June Gillam

THE END OF THIS FIRST EDITION OF *WRITING IN SMALL GROUPS THE 4COLOR WAY*.

PLEASE GO TO <u>WWW.JUNEGILLAM.COM</u> AND REPLY TO MAKE SUGGESTIONS FOR CHANGES FOR THE SECOND EDITION.

I THANK YOU KINDLY FOR YOUR ASSISTANCE!

JUNE GILLAM
<u>jgillam@deltacollege.edu</u>
Gorilla Girl Ink
gorillagirlink@gmail.com